IDEAS Plus

A Collection of Practical Teaching Ideas

Book Five

National Council of Teachers of English
1111 Kenyon Road, Urbana, Illinois 61801

Staff Editor: Felice A. Kaufmann

Book Design: Tom Kovacs for TGK Design

Illustrator: Richard Maul

NCTE Stock Number 22515

Library of Congress Catalog Card Number 84-3479

Contents

Foreword

IDEAS Plus and its quarterly companion *NOTES Plus* are the principal benefits of NCTE Plus membership. *IDEAS Plus* is sent out at the end of the summer so that teachers will have it in hand as they begin the school year.

This fifth edition of *IDEAS Plus* was assembled primarily from the ideas submitted at the Idea Exchange sessions at NCTE Annual Conventions and the recent Spring Conference.

1 Language Exploration

In the world of words, the imagination is one of the forces of nature.

Wallace Stevens

Learning to use the power and resources of the imagination will help students master the world of words, as will the teaching strategies described in this section on language exploration. Students experience many different facets of language in these activities, in which they examine the subjectivity of magazine news reports, invent new words and definitions, prepare and present consumer reports on popular products, and give talks based on personal field trips.

Know Your News

Here's an exercise that makes students more conscious of the subjectivity of language. Our school librarian helps me prepare for this assignment by putting together a set of magazines for each student. Each set contains three newsmagazines from the same week: one copy of *Time,* one copy of *Newsweek,* and one copy of *U.S. News and World Report.*

Each student receives one set of magazines and several copies of a worksheet on which he or she notes the following:

subject of story

amount of coverage in each magazine

location of story in each magazine

loaded words used

Students use one worksheet per news story and can usually complete two or three in a class period.

Because each student works with magazines from a different week, I ask students to share some of their findings with the rest of the class.

I encourage students to describe the impact of specific words and phrases found in their articles. Using an example where the three sources differ noticeably in coverage, we talk about what conclusions a reader might draw after reading only one account and what conclusions the reader might draw after reading all three.

I use this assignment after teaching a unit on propaganda, so my students usually have a lot to say about how subtle differences in news articles could influence readers. This assignment could also be tied in to a unit on advertising techniques or to a discussion of connotation and denotation.

Frances DeLamater, Roy C. Start High School, Toledo, Ohio

Sniglets and Snickerettes

For the past year my students have been enjoying the *Sniglets* calendar on the wall of our classroom. *Sniglets,* originated by Rich Hall, are amusing made-up words and definitions. For example, a *gyroped* is "a kid who cannot resist spinning around on a diner stool." I use a variation on the *sniglet* as part of our study of word parts and using the thesaurus.

Each student needs a thesaurus, preferably one in which the entries are listed alphabetically, and a list of common prefixes, suffixes, and root words. (Many textbooks contain such a list.) After distributing these resources, I explain briefly how information is organized in the thesaurus, have students look up a few words for practice, and review the word parts on the handout sheet.

Next I tell students that we are going to create "snickerettes"—an adaptation of the sniglet. I ask students to brainstorm for frustrating or ironic situations that seem to warrant their own descriptive terms, such as "the sudden plummet in temperature after you leave home without a jacket." I list all students' suggestions on the chalkboard.

When students run out of ideas, it's time to invent words to match our definitions. Making a sack lunch and forgetting it at home was dubbed "hamnesia" by my students. The attraction of large, muddy canines to light-colored clothing was termed "pastelmagnetization." After creating a half dozen or so "snickerettes" as a group, students will be ready to work individually.

I check on students periodically to make sure they understand how to use their references. The thesaurus gives students a choice of uncommon synonyms to use in their definitions and also provides models for how to word a definition. The list of prefixes, suffixes, and root words helps students create words that sound authentic. Two examples of students' work are shown below:

> *Quizfibrillation:* when the realization that you have a test hits you just as you enter the classroom
>
> *Scotthesion:* the tendency of the last sheet of toilet paper to cling to the roll

Susan Adcox, Barters Hill High School, Mont Belvieu, Texas

Consumers Report

Most teenagers are just beginning to be "conscious consumers," becoming aware for the first time that similar products often vary widely in cost and quality. Here's a project that does double duty for consumer awareness and language skills. Students test and review selected products, write evaluative reports, and present their findings to the class.

To begin, I bring a stack of back issues of *Consumer Reports* to class. I ask students to skim through them and notice the format and style of product reviews. We talk about the different types of tests performed on products, the care taken to test each product in the same way, the graphs and tables that help explain the researchers' findings, and the way the reviewers sum up their views of the products.

Then I give the assignment: to review and report on a product in the manner of *Consumer Reports.* Since students will need to buy from four to six different brands of the product chosen, I help them think of inexpensive possibilities, preferably items that they will have some use for after the testing. My students generally settle on such products as bubble gum, felt-tip pens, dish detergent, nail polish remover, hamburgers, soft drinks, potato chips, and so on. Students may choose only products that can be reviewed adequately without special knowledge or equipment.

Each student decides the criteria by which to evaluate his or her product, using at least four criteria. For a dishwashing liquid, possible criteria might include price, amount of suds generated, lasting quality of suds, gentleness on skin, color, and fragrance. I allot time for in-class research where necessary, as in opinion surveys concerning taste.

After students test their products, they write up their findings in report form, modeling their writing on the reviews in *Consumer Reports.* Each report should include:

an introduction

a description of the product

a list of the brands tested

a description of the tests

a detailed summary of the findings, including an explanation of any special considerations (such as "These potato chips weren't as crisp as the other brands, but I bought this bag on sale. It's possible that the only reason these chips aren't as crisp is that this bag has been around longer than the others.")

recommendations (such as "This detergent is harsh on hands, but it's much cheaper than the others and gets high ratings in other categories. If you don't mind wearing rubber gloves while you wash dishes, this brand might be worth buying.")

at least one chart or graph displaying test results

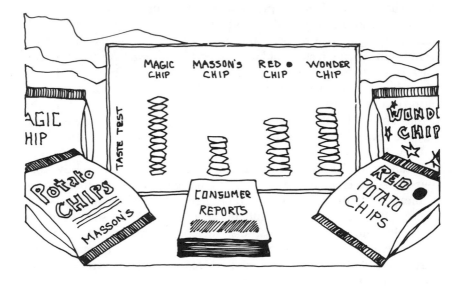

Students enjoy all phases of this project. Most students are very thorough in their testing and in keeping track of the results, and many find imaginative ways to back their claims with visual aids. A student presenter might pass around anything from instant photos showing the "suds' lasting power" of various dish soaps to a row of potato chips glued to a piece of cardboard showing thickness and color. After all the reports have been presented, I display the charts and visual aids in a corner of the classroom to remind students what they have learned about careful consumerism.

Doris Hickman, Shelbina, Missouri

Personal Field Trips

For the most part, English teachers today inform students of the world outside the school via textbooks, films, videos, and occasional guest speakers. The field trip as a teaching tool is losing out to technology. Where once whole classes might have visited a city theater or a university playhouse to see *Macbeth,* now *Macbeth* comes into the classroom in a can.

It is easier to schedule an in-class film than to schedule a group field trip, but there's a way to offer students the benefits of out-of-class learning without chartering a bus or disrupting the daily schedule.

I capitalize on my students' lives outside the classroom to enrich their learning in the classroom, making use of activities that students probably consider diversions rather than learning situations. Each student is required to take four "personal field trips" during the school year and, after each trip, to present an oral report three to five minutes in length to the class. An added benefit is that students can enjoy the field trips of their classmates by listening to and commenting on their reports.

There is no limit, except that of available time, to the number of personal field trips and reports that students may make during the year. I encourage students to think of the ways in which each trip was interesting or valuable to them. After a trip, students might be asked to imagine that they are teachers proposing the same trip to school administrators as a class field trip, and to give all the reasons they can think of to justify the school's expense.

Listed below are examples of the kinds of trips I suggest to my students. Other options might include anything from a tour of a factory, foundry, or business to a nature walk in a state or national park.

1. Visit the public library.
2. Accompany a classmate of a different faith or denomination than your own to a service in his or her church, synogogue, or meeting place.
3. Visit Bath, North Carolina, the oldest city in the state.
4. See a play in Taylor Theater at Campbell University.
5. Visit the Thomas Wolfe House in Asheville.
6. Attend a play, a dance performance, or a lecture in Turner Auditorium at Methodist College.
7. See *The Nutcracker Suite* in Memorial Auditorium.
8. Visit The Folger Library in Washington, D.C.
9. Visit Winston-Salem.

10. Visit Fort Bragg Playhouse.
11. Visit the North Carolina Museum of Art in Raleigh.
12. See an outdoor drama, such as *Strike at the Wind, Lost Colony,* or *Blackbeard's Revenge.*

Lloyd Chambers, Autryville, North Carolina

The Do's and Don'ts of Study Skills

I've had a lot of difficulty motivating one particular group of eighth graders. When it came time to teach study skills, I realized that something had to be done. This was subject matter they could ill afford to let "fly in one ear and out the other." Knowing from experience that the best way to learn something is to teach it, I devised this assignment.

I asked students to imagine that they had befriended a Martian teenager just recently arrived on Earth. This new friend had no knowledge of study skills and needed their help in order to survive the eighth grade. The assignment was to make a videotape to teach their friend a necessary skill. Each group of four or five students chose one of the following topics:

1. The do's and don'ts of taking notes in class
2. The do's and don'ts of taking notes from a book
3. The do's and don'ts of studying at home
4. The do's and don'ts of test-taking skills

The videotapes were to cover the material we had talked about in class. I asked students to exercise their creativity and make their video presentations not only informative but interesting.

We all had reason to be happy with the final results. Some groups provided musical accompaniment and others made "silent films," but all the videotapes presented the material in a fresh and interesting way. The school gained a valuable resource (the tapes are now used by the special education teacher), and my students learned valuable skills while in the role of the teacher.

Rae Hansen, Pierce High School, Pierce, Nebraska

Scrutinizing Success

Many of the students I teach suffer from poor self-images. With little confidence in themselves or in their ability to read, write, or speak well, how can these students hope to find even limited success in high school English?

A major goal of my English program is to improve students' opinions of themselves, which I do in part by helping them focus on their successes and accomplishments. The following unit, which I developed with Pat Fletcher (Harry Ainlay Composite High), prompts students to acknowledge personal achievements both large and small, to explore what success means to different people, and to gain confidence through conducting interviews and speaking in front of a group.

I begin by explaining that we are going to explore the concept of success. I tell students that I believe many of us think of success only in terms of grand achievements and don't give ourselves credit for the things we learn and accomplish every day. I ask students to begin a series of journal entries in which they record all the "successes" they experience during the term, no matter how small. I keep track of my own successes as well. Periodically during the unit we take time to read aloud selected entries to the rest of the class. The following are examples of entries my students have read:

"I got to class on time"

"I did my homework"

"I figured out what was wrong when my parents' car didn't start this morning"

"I got a date with _____ from math class"

"I had a grade of 78% on the English test"

"I found an after-school job"

As a class we spend a week or two exploring and discussing works of literature and films that offer glimpses at the successes of others:

"The Verger" by W. Somerset Maugham (short story)

"The Moth and the Star" by James Thurber (fable)

"Warren Pryor" by Alden Nowlan (poem)

Norma Rae starring Sally Field (movie)

Related writing assignments ask students to compare the different meanings success has for different people.

Then, to complement writing and reading, I assign an oral report based on success. My handout of instructions to students is shown below.

Your assignment is to give an oral presentation on the meaning of success, using information gathered from five interviews.

Step One: What is your current definition of success? Write it out in detail and then set it aside for the moment.

Step Two: Decide on the focus of your presentation. You may choose to base your oral report on either a general or a specific discussion of success, and you will need to choose the people you interview accordingly. For example, if you decide to focus on personal qualities that can make a person successful in any field, you might interview people of various ages and from a variety of backgrounds with diverse work experience. Or, for a more narrow approach, you might interview only parents and develop a definition of what constitutes success for a parent.

Step Three: Interview five people who you think are successful in the chosen field. (Of these five, only one can be a member of your family.)

Step Four: Arrange the time and place of each interview beforehand. Explain the assignment to the person, including why you want to interview him or her. If possible, give each person you are interviewing a day or two to reflect before the interview.

Step Five: Prepare a list of questions ahead of time. Phrase your questions so that you don't offend the person you interview. (Instead of asking, "So, how much money are you making?" you might ask, "Are you satisfied with your income?") Use follow-up questions to find out further details.

Remember to thank your interviewee for his or her time and input. As a further courtesy, you may wish to send a card expressing your appreciation.

Step Six: After you have conducted five interviews, spend several days preparing your oral presentation.

Look back at your first definition of success to see whether your thoughts have changed as a result of readings, class discussions, and interviews. Is your view of what constitutes success any broader (or narrower) than it was before? What is your current opinion of what makes a person successful?

Next decide on an appropriate organization for your information (which questions/responses will be presented first, which last?) and order (whose responses will be presented first, whose last?) Prepare your notes as simply and legibly as possible.

Use the introduction to explain your topic, give your original definition of success, and name the five people whom you interviewed (first names, ages, occupations. . .). In the course of your presentation, tell why you chose to interview each person you did and summarize what he or she said about success in general and about his or her own success. In your conclusion, tell the class whether or not your view of success has changed as a result of your research, and if so, how.

Remember: when you give your presentation, don't *read* your notes; *refer* to them.

Obviously this unit alone cannot be expected to raise students' self-esteem, but it can help students appreciate their own accomplishments and recognize the many different criteria by which people evaluate themselves and their success.

Cameron C. Fahlman, McNally Composite High School, Edmonton, Alberta

Sports Page Close-Up

Here's a simple way to get students talking about language, in this case the language used in the sports section of the daily newspaper. I ask students to collect sports sections from several different newspapers over the course of a week and to bring them to class. Then I distribute copies of the list of questions below. I ask students to spend ten or fifteen minutes reading through the questions and jotting down their answers. Then we discuss their answers in class.

List all the synonyms for *win* or *defeat* you can find on the first page of the sports section.

What are the connotations of each synonym? Do the synonyms used give you an idea of how close the score was or how the teams played?

Are any synonyms chosen to tie in to the names of the teams? For example, is a verb ordinarily associated with an animal used with an animal team name?

What do the teams' names mean? What qualities are associated with each name? Are there any team names that suggest the industry or history of the home city?

How do headlines resemble and differ from sentences? From book or movie titles? What is omitted and why?

Students enjoy poring over the sports page looking for the answers to these questions, and our discussion ensures that they will look more closely at what they read the next time they pick up a newspaper.

Carolyn Hartnett, College of the Mainland, Texas City, Texas

Vocabulary Madness

Several years ago, when sophomores at our school scored poorly on the PSAT's and other standardized tests, our guidance counselor recommended that I concentrate on improving the vocabulary of my freshman students. I readily agreed, believing inwardly that this could not be too difficult.

Armed with a vocabulary textbook, I began to assign lists of twenty words on Mondays, to hold discussions on any problems on Wednesdays, and to give vocabulary quizzes on Fridays. My students did well on the quizzes, but I soon found that although students were able to memorize words for a quiz, those words were forgotten by the end of the following week. A new plan was needed.

I then began requiring students to write and hand in sentences using the assigned words, but again I found that there was no long-range retention of the words. A workbook became my next course of action, as the months and my patience began to slip by. But the workbook introduced words that students didn't see or hear again, so there was little reinforcement once students memorized the words. Had I actually once believed that teaching vocabulary would be easy? I must have been mad!

Fortunately, as I continued in desperation to experiment, a successful vocabulary teaching method finally emerged out of my madness. My students groan and moan when I explain it, but they later admit that they know a lot more words than they did when we started.

The strength of this rather simple method is the extent to which it involves students in the learning process. Every night I assign three words, each in the context of a sentence. Students keep a notebook in which the words and the given sentences are written. For homework, students are to find the meaning and the part of speech for each word and to write an original sentence using each word. Students are also to spend some time reviewing previous words. Each day's lesson begins with a discussion of the words, clarification of meanings and connotations, sharing of sentences, and, most importantly, a quick, random review of previous words.

This method serves several purposes. First of all, since my students have a vocabulary assignment every night, they learn slowly but surely, rather than being faced with a long list of words to memorize for a test at the end of the quarter. Secondly, beginning each day's lesson with a discussion of the words gives me immediate control of my class. Students know what to expect and are ready to begin right away. This method also promotes independent studying, which my freshmen may not be used to. I don't collect the notebooks; it is students' responsibility to keep them up-to-date. (Occasional open-notebook quizzes encourage diligence in this area.)

Wise choice of vocabulary words is crucial to student learning. I want students to learn words that will be genuinely useful to them, and ones that will be continually reinforced by the media and their own reading. I compile a long list of words from newspapers, television, radio, novels, and short stories. Another idea is to search magazines and novels popular with teenagers to find words that they might not know, or to copy from teen magazines or novels sentences containing common words and to introduce less common, more powerful synonyms for these words.

Students have a standing invitation to share with the class any encounters they have with the new words they have learned. Whether it's *altercation* heard on the evening news or *impunity* discovered in a history textbook, students are always delighted to come across words they have learned. In fact, I consider this as perhaps the most important factor in motivating students to continue learning new words. My students not only keep a lookout for the words they've learned, but they begin to use such new words as *emulate* and *commiserate* confidently and correctly in their writing and conversation.

I generally choose the three words for a particular day in the following way. The first word always has a root that the students must learn. I doubt that my students could or would remember a list of roots for very long, but when each root is taught in the context of a word, students have a much easier time remembering each one. For example, if the first word for the day is *malign,* students are also responsible for knowing that "mal" means "bad." When I later give them the word *malevolent,* they are able to make the connection between the two words and can often guess at the meaning. For the second word of the day, I choose a word students will later come across in one of our literature selections. The third word is simply a word chosen from one of the sources mentioned earlier—books, magazines, or newspapers— or even chosen from one of the vocabulary books I acquired during my pre-method days.

Since reinforcement and review are so important, I often do quick oral vocabulary reviews, especially when I have a spare minute or two at the end of a class period. I also devote a corner of the chalkboard to vocabulary words, where I copy down new words and review older ones. Of course, the real beauty of this method is that much of the review takes place when students encounter the words outside of the classroom.

Karen Geiger, St. Peter's High School, Mansfield, Ohio

Punctuation in Practice

After working for what seemed like an eternity on punctuation, particularly on the use of direct and indirect quotes, we took a break to read "The Kitten" by Richard Wright. In the ensuing discussion about the family's many problems, we talked about the great anger and frustration displayed by the father, and how the young boy's mother must have felt in such a hopeless situation. One student pointed out that when people are angry, they often say things that they don't mean and that they later regret.

Suddenly I thought of a follow-up writing exercise that would incorporate some much-needed practice with punctuation. I asked students, "How many of you while growing up heard the statement, 'If I've told you once, I've told you a thousand times . . .'?" Immediately the room began to buzz. It seemed that everyone could remember a situation in which a family member or friend had become angry or frustrated and used this phrase. Students began to laugh and compare notes on their memories.

Building on this, I asked students to write a short dialogue between two people in which one uses the phrase "If I've told you once, I've told you a thousand times. . . ." I told students that I would be looking especially closely for correct use of quotation marks.

Students worked on their dialogues in class for two days. When they finished writing, we reviewed punctuation rules and students made any necessary corrections. The final products were outstanding. I was surprised at the number of students who wanted to read their dialogues aloud before handing them in.

Mary-Sue Gardetto, Ankeney Junior High School, Beavercreek, Ohio

Eye-Catching Errors

We've all seen advertisements that use deliberate errors to attract the eye. Catchy slogans may include shortened words, phonetically spelled words, misplaced apostrophes, or lack of agreement between subject and verb. Examples can be found everywhere—in newspapers, magazines, road signs, TV commercials, comic books, yellow pages, and store and restaurant names. The following assignment highlights this common advertising technique while sharpening students' sensitivity to errors.

I ask students to find as many examples of nonstandard spelling and grammar in advertising as they can. Ads from magazines may be clipped out; examples from television ads, billboards, store fronts, and so on may be copied down (along with the source, to encourage honesty). After a few days of searching, students share their findings with the class. Each student is to read aloud his or her slogans and phrases and to explain where the error lies in each one. In the past, students have cited such examples as "Star-kist," "Cure your window pains," and "Them's eatin' words." The resulting list of slogans and phrases on the chalkboard provides a natural lead-in to a discussion of wordplay, personification, and symbolism in advertising.

As the final step in this activity, I ask students to use "creative" spelling and grammar in slogans of their own, advertising either real or imaginary products. They spend a day thinking and writing and then read aloud to the class such slogans as "It's the third annual Boat Show Sailabration!" and "John's Fishing Rods—they're the reel thing."

Mary Castle, Ketchikan, Alaska

Teacher Talks

In this activity, students hear a formal talk in which a member of the faculty, administration, or staff speaks on how and for what he or she would like to be remembered.

I use this activity every three or four years and usually schedule five or six talks for the last month of the school year. They are scheduled to take place in the classroom unless a particularly large audience is expected, in which case I reserve the choral room. (With permission of the speaker, other faculty or outsiders are sometimes invited.) Potential speakers are usually flattered to be asked. But be forewarned that administrators sometimes find it difficult to schedule time and may occasionally cancel at the last minute.

I ask speakers to prepare talks that last approximately forty-five minutes so that students have time for questions at the end. A student volunteer introduces the speaker, using facts that the speaker provides ahead of time, and another student volunteer thanks the speaker after the last question and the speaker's closing remarks.

These talks tend to surprise students by showing them glimpses into the private lives of people they know only on a superficial level. Two of the most interesting speeches given in my class include one by a custodian who was a Hitler expert and who brought in a display of Nazi artifacts, and another by an attendance clerk who used to work at MGM. Students are prompted to consider what they themselves might want to accomplish in their lives; a natural follow-up to this activity is a discussion of career choices.

Bill Corey, Antioch High School, Antioch, California

Time Capsule

I use this idea with seventh graders, but I'm sure it could be adapted for students at other levels.

On the first day of the school year, I ask my new seventh graders, who are starting a six-year career at a junior/senior high school, to brainstorm impressions of their first day. They describe their thoughts about encountering a strange building, new teachers and students, unfamiliar courses, and so on. On the second day we review the comments from the previous day, and students write down a one- or two-page description of their first day of junior high. I collect these papers; they are destined for our time capsule.

Several weeks later, after students have settled in, I bring a large box to class. A dishwasher box from a local appliance store works well. Questions fly as everyone wonders what the box is for. I explain that the box is a time capsule; it will store memories of this year and enable students to look back as high school seniors and remember what it was like to be a seventh grader. (The time capsule could be opened at the end of one or two years, but the effect is much more dramatic if the wait is longer.)

The next day, students each bring to class a shoe box or a box of similar size. I ask them to include a few items of personal memorabilia (excluding items of value) that they would like to find upon opening the box as seniors, such as a concert ticket stub, a favorite cartoon, or a napkin autographed by a friend. These individual boxes are placed inside the time capsule, which I then store somewhere safe but accessible. Students in this year's class covered the outside of the time capsule with favorite sayings and signatures. In other years, students have drawn and painted scenes on the outside.

Besides the spontaneous contributions that students make during the year, I periodically ask students to donate a particular item or assignment to the time capsule. I choose assignments that I think students will find amusing or interesting when older. The following is a list of some assignments that have ended up in our time capsule.

1. We include the students' first compositions of the year: impressions of the first day of junior high.

2. At our open house I ask each student's parent or guardian to write a short letter to the student and place it in the student's box. I ask students whose parents or guardian didn't attend to bring in a short letter from home, and I put it in their boxes.

3. Each student draws a name from a hat and writes a cinquain and an acrostic poem about the student whose name was drawn.

After the poems are read aloud, they go in the boxes of their namesakes.

4. Each student's height is measured, and a string of the same length is placed in his or her box in the time capsule.

5. As a class we determine a "Who's Who" list, designating one student as friendliest, one as best actor, one as having the best memory, one as most patient, and so on. Copies go in the time capsule.

6. Students fill out interest inventory sheets, detailing their hobbies, interests, and goals, and place a copy in the time capsule.

7. I take a class photograph and include it in the time capsule. Students also have the option of placing snapshots of themselves in their boxes.

8. We include a cassette on which I and my students record one-minute messages to our future selves.

9. Scripts for skits and commercials written and performed by students are photocopied and included.

When students' senior year rolls around, we have a group reunion and open the time capsule. Students reminisce with much laughter as they read poems written about them by their classmates, hear their own voices giving them advice from the past, locate themselves in a six-year-old group photo, and measure themselves with strings that, in some cases, now reach only shoulder high.

Alicia L. Cross, Hopkinton High School, Contoocook, New Hampshire

Commemorative Ceremonies

As we teach our students about literary and historical people and events that have made a difference in our world in some way, we may sometimes sense that students are learning only names and dates—that the greater significance is being lost. How can we communicate to students the full impact of these lives and events?

I recently introduced commemorative ceremonies in my seventh-grade English classes. On the first anniversary of the death of the *Challenger* astronauts, seventh-grade students in each class vied for the honor of holding or lighting candles in memory of the astronauts. When these classes commemorated the birthday of Martin Luther King, Jr., the five available speaking parts in a student-written tribute were so hotly contested that we finally determined them by random drawing.

Those who were not chosen for a part demanded advance priority in the next tribute.

After witnessing enthusiastic responses like these, I would recommend this strategy as a way to deepen students' involvement in the study of literature and history. Commemorative ceremonies can be equally effective whether held for contemporary figures such as those mentioned above or for figures from the past, such as William Shakespeare, Emily Dickinson, Ralph Waldo Emerson, Mahatma Gandhi, Harriet Tubman, and others.

After selecting an individual or event to commemorate, I usually suggest that we hold the ceremony on the individual's birthday, or on the designated national holiday if there is one. For our study of such contemporary figures as Martin Luther King, Jr., John F. Kennedy, and the *Challenger* astronauts, my students interview their parents, community members, relatives, and peers to find out their impressions of these individuals' lives and accomplishments. Among the questions students ask in interviews are:

> Where were you and what were you doing when you heard about the death of this person?
>
> What was your first reaction?
>
> In what ways did this person touch your life?
>
> What do you feel was this person's most significant contribution to society?

Students' research, reading, and reflection create the raw material for the commemorative ceremony. In the course of reading, students take notes from writings by and about the individual. I frequently remind students not to look for facts and dates, but to think in broader terms, considering such questions as:

> What was this person trying to do with his or her life?
>
> Were his or her goals accomplished?
>
> What influence did his or her life and work have on others at the time?
>
> What effect is this person's life still having on us today?

While reading, students extract what they feel are significant quotations made by or about the individual and write their reactions to these statements. They also locate pictures and photographs for display in the classroom and for use in the ceremony. Such pictures serve as inspiration for student artists to paint or draw their own images of the person.

Finally, students reflect and write their final thoughts on the impact of the individual's life and work for the rest of the world. Meeting in groups, students review and evaluate materials, and with some advice from me, they make a final selection of the readings for the ceremony, which may be scheduled to last anywhere from ten minutes to an entire class period.

Here is an outline illustrating one possible way to organize a twenty- or thirty-minute ceremony.

1. Speaker One describes the person or event inspiring the tribute.

2. Speaker Two gives the background for the project—what tasks were involved, what resources were used, and so on.

3. Speaker Three and as many other speakers as are needed read selected portions from students' writings (interviews, reactions to writings about the person or event, and so on) and selected passages from other writings by or about the person or about the event.

4. The final speaker closes the ceremony by reading from a student's reflection on the significance of the subject's life or the event and how it affects students today. He or she then lights one or more candles, after which we observe a moment of silence in commemoration of the person or event.

In the course of preparing a commemorative ceremony, students practice research, reading, notetaking, interviewing, analysis, writing, and speaking. Further, in celebrating the accomplishments of people from a variety of different fields, students gain a sense for the possibilities in their own lives.

Rose Reissman, Ditmas Junior High, Brooklyn, New York

Thinking Ahead

I like to ask my seventh graders to think about their futures and how they would like to be remembered, but having students write their own obituaries has always seemed a bit ghoulish to me. While visiting relatives over the Christmas holidays, I found an article in the local newspaper that listed famous people who had died in 1986, giving me an idea for a more positive teaching strategy.

I pared down the newspaper's list to the shorter one shown below.

Desi Arnaz	W. Averell Harriman
Ted Knight	Candido Jacuzzi
Len Bias	Henry Moore
James Cagney	Georgia O'Keeffe
Norm Cash	Otto Preminger
John Ciardi	Donna Reed
Broderick Crawford	Admiral Hyman Rickover
Scatman Crothers	William Schroeder
Perry Ellis	Francis Scobee
Dr. Rudolf Flesch	Kate Smith
Benny Goodman	Rudy Vallee
Cary Grant	Bill Veeck
Florence Halop	Theodore White

I distributed copies of this list to my students and asked them to see how many of the names they could identify. Students had a great time repeating the names aloud and trying to remember what they knew about each person. Our discussion included a lot of guessing—some intelligent and some wild. I listened to all the speculation but refused to confirm or deny students' guesswork.

At the end of the class period, I asked students to find out the identity of every person on the list, using any resources available to them. The next day, I awarded prizes to the students who had come up with the most information. We discussed the interesting facts that students had obtained and their methods of finding out what they did. The most popular resources included:

  the card catalog of the local library

  Who's Who in America (Marquis, annual)

The Filmgoer's Companion, Leslie Halliwell, ed. (Hill and Wang, 1977)

The International Motion Picture Almanac (Quigley, annual)

Musicians Since 1900, David Ewen (Wilson, 1978)

Teachers, parents, and friends were also popular sources for any light they could shed on the identities of the names on the list.

As we discussed the careers and talents for which the people on the list would be remembered, I found it natural to move the discussion to what students themselves would like to accomplish in their lifetimes. I accepted comments from everyone in the class, and then announced a topic for a short writing assignment: "How I Would Like the World to Remember Me."

Linda Marquardt, Watertown Junior High School, Watertown, South Dakota

Family Lore and More

Research isn't something students ordinarily rave about, but they are more likely to show interest when the subject of investigation is the history of their own families and of the area in which they live. As students complete assignments, they compile the results in book form. (Items that cannot be included in a book may be shared with the class in some other way.) By the end of the project, each has a "keepsake" book filled with family lore and local history.

Just before Thanksgiving I hand out the list of assignments given below and talk briefly with students about possible procedures and resources. I ask students to turn in their finished books during the week after Christmas vacation, giving them the opportunity to work on the project with their families and allowing enough time to produce quality results. (Students whose family situations prevent them from researching family ancestry or other family information can focus on assignments involving local history and traditions of the area.)

I ask students to complete nine of the fourteen assignments listed below.

1. Interview a member of your extended family who is at least two generations older than you (or conduct the same interview with an unrelated older person). Your goal is to find out "the way it was." Ask for as much biographical information as possible: full name, date and place of birth, all the places where the individual has lived, occupation (former, if retired), and so

on. You are free to explore any other topics that you find interesting, such as family life, transportation, housing, clothing, hairstyles, entertainment, games, songs, dating, vacations, books, movies, and education. Record the interview on a cassette tape and make a pocket for the cassette on a page of your book. Make a written copy of the interview as well.

2. If you have an ancestor who moved to America from another country, find out as much as you can about his or her life. Write a three- to four-page account of your ancestor's arrival in America, explaining "who, why, when, and where." Feel free to add fictional details as needed. Cite your sources. As an alternative to writing about an ancestor, write a three- to four-page factual account of your immediate family's move to this area. Explain why and when your family moved here. Cite your sources.

3. Write a three- to four-page biography of one of your ancestors or of a historical figure who was prominent in the development of this region. Cite your sources.

4. Research and draw your own family tree for the last three generations, or research and draw the family tree of a family prominent in the history of the area. Include a short biographical profile for each entry wherever possible.

5. Locate an old home with a historical marker. Write a three- to four-page history of the home. Add fictional details as needed. Include at least two photographs or drawings of the home. Cite your sources.

6. Make two gravestone rubbings from stones dated no later than 1930. Also record the information from the stones on a separate piece of paper, including the name and location of the cemetery. (Suggested resource: "Making Tombstone Rubbings a Work of Art," *Southern Living,* July 1976, 64-65.)

7. Make something that was unavailable for purchase a few generations ago, such as bread, soap, dye, a wooden toy, a crocheted or knitted article, a patchwork square from a traditional design, a candle, a clay bowl or pitcher, preserved food, or a leather belt, pouch, or purse. Prepare a simplified written explanation of the steps involved. Display your finished product for the class and explain how you made it.

8. Visit a historic site in the state. Take at least twelve photographs and arrange, mount, and label each with a description of its significance.

9. Visit a local or state museum or a library collection that displays items relating to the history of the area. Collect pamphlets about the display and mount them in your book. Prepare a page describing the exhibit and giving the location and hours of the museum or display.

10. Write a poem of at least twenty lines using any rhyme scheme or form. The subject of the poem may be either your family or a historical event of regional interest. In your book, include a draft and a final version of the poem.

11. Collect ten favorite family recipes, or ten recipes that are typical of this region of the country. Include a copy of each recipe in your book and explain the significance of each. Answer such questions as:

    Where did the recipe originate?

    At what times of year is it prepared?

    On what special occasions might it be served?

    What else is it usually served with?

12. Draw or paint a scene from your family's past or an event from regional history, using any medium (pencil, chalk, watercolors, etc.).

13. Take a photograph of each member of your family, including yourself. Or visit a local family business, explain your assignment, and take a photograph of the family members who work in the business. Write a character description to accompany each photograph.

14. In a cigar box or shoe box, create a time capsule of family items and set a certain date to open it, such as a holiday five, ten, or twenty years from now. Include at least ten items. Plan a safe place to store your box. Write a detailed list of what you include and why, and put this list in your book. As an alternative to items associated with your family, you could also find items uniquely associated with the community—a matchbook from a well-known local restaurant, a guide to local parks, a postcard of the courthouse, a ticket stub from a ball game, and so on.

As the final step in this project, everyone designs a cover for his or her keepsake book. To match the mood of our research and writing, I encourage students to use photographs or illustrations that depict family memories or regional history.

Karen Werkenthin, Georgetown High School, Georgetown, Texas

An Answer to the Overloaded File Cabinet

We all get great ideas from many sources, including journals, teacher conferences, and co-workers. Frequently, however, we don't need those ideas right at that moment. What can you do with the perfect idea to ensure that you can put your hands on it when you need it? And another thing—how do you organize the multiple copies of tests and handouts, the unit and lesson plans, and scraps of paper bearing essential notes, all of which accumulate in overwhelming proportions after just a few years of teaching?

The suggestion offered by Dianne Robinson in the November 1983 issue of *NOTES Plus* is a start. For several years now I have done just what she suggested—put all my information into notebooks. This idea works well and I highly recommend it, but I would like to make a suggestion that takes the idea one step further—the unit box.

The unit box is nothing more than a heavy cardboard box. (I find that the boxes that hold ten reams of paper are ideal and readily available around a school.) Into this box I deposit absolutely everything that I need for a single unit. The idea sounds obvious, but it can really make a difference.

I teach seven units—the short story, the novel, modern drama, Shakespeare, poetry, writing instruction, and the research paper. In years past I have used notebooks for papers and then had to find room in drawers, closets, and cubby holes for all the materials that wouldn't fit in a notebook. I frequently forgot about some wonderful resource I might have used—a cassette tape of poetry, a poster, a calendar—because it was out of sight and out of mind.

This year when a unit was completed, I gathered up literally everything that related to the unit and threw it all into a box. For instance, in my short story box I placed the following:

    photocopied short stories not found in our text

    photocopied handouts that had been used as class copies

    books on teaching the short story

    pamphlets

    cassettes of taped short stories

    videocassettes of short stories

    interest items such as a purple rabbit's foot for "The Monkey's Paw"

    transparencies explaining the elements of a short story

    bulletin board materials (letters, pictures, and so on, plus an instant photograph of the completed display) an idea notebook listing everything I wasn't currently using to teach the unit but might want to use in the future

a course notebook containing specific content material for each class, copies of and notes for short stories, and tests, both daily and major

a major notebook containing everything needed to teach the unit including unit plans, daily plans, notes on films, handout masters, masters of photocopied stories, notes on all input, and a list of all available A.V. materials in the library or service center

The nicest thing about using a unit box is that whenever I come across something I believe will be useful for a particular unit, I just drop it into the box. I make no attempt to file it at that time. When I get ready to teach the unit, I go through everything in the box, sort it, and file it. I then can make up my unit knowing that I have considered all my possible resources. The box I use is easy to store and easy to carry home when I need to prepare the unit.

The hardest part of this plan is just doing it. Don't try to convert everything at once. Instead, as you teach each unit this year, begin to gather up and drop everything for that unit into a box. By the end of the year, most of your work will have been done. Then you can stop promising yourself that this is the year you'll get organized.

Susan E. L. Lake, Lubbock-Cooper High School, Lubbock, Texas

2 Literature

What we learn with pleasure, we never forget.

Alfred Mercier

The lessons that literature has to teach are countless, but as we all know, the atmosphere in the classroom can be an important factor in how well a lesson is learned. Try using the following ideas to stimulate interest in the study of literature and to make students more receptive to the benefits of what they read. The recommended assignments will help students understand the importance of the oral history of *Beowulf,* predict what might happen next in a novel, analyze an author's style, compose letters based on "The Rape of the Lock," write an additional episode for H. G. Wells's time traveler, and develop conversations about a novel read out of class.

Beowulf and "The Three Little Pigs"

When introducing a work of literature, I am always looking for innovative ways to capture student attention as well as to make a point. Before beginning *Beowulf,* I ask my senior British literature students to write the story of "The Three Little Pigs." After the moaning and complaining subside, students begin the task. I generally allow about twenty minutes for writing, and then students read their accounts aloud.

What initially appeared to be a story that everyone knows by heart turns out to have some very interesting differences depending on who is telling the story. Each student remembers one detail more than another, particularly in regard to the pigs' purpose in building their homes and the outcome of the wolf. Lively debate follows such questions as:

Where is the pigs' father?

Why did the pigs leave home?

Where did the pigs get the materials to build their houses?

30

At this point I introduce *Beowulf,* stressing the importance of its oral history, the anonymous author, and the changes that undoubtedly occurred in the original story as it was passed from generation to generation. Students are surprised to learn that "The Three Little Pigs" is a British folktale probably dating back to the Anglo-Saxons and that it, too, has an anonymous author.

I have found that this strategy for introducing *Beowulf* increases students' understanding and appreciation of the epic poem tremendously.

N. Denise Burke, Wheatland High School, Wyoming

A Nonthreatening Guide to Any Novel

When journal writing had proven to be a nonthreatening activity to engage students in getting thoughts onto paper, I wondered if focused freewritings could also help reluctant readers as they were reading a novel for a book report. Almost unconsciously, good readers *predict* what might happen on the next page or in the next chapter. I prepared a few guided freewriting questions to help less practiced readers predict—and therefore think—more about their books.

Before students selected their novels, I distributed a handout with the following guidelines:

Five Writings Based on Your Chosen Novel
(to be completed as you read the book)

1. *Before you begin reading:* React to the title of the book. What might it mean? What does it make you think of? Tell why you picked this book to read. What expectations do you have?

2. *After reading the first chapter:* Predict what you think is going to happen in the rest of the book, and explain why you think so. (Correctness doesn't count here; just make an educated guess, an honest speculation about what might follow.)

3. *When you are halfway through the book:* Summarize the problems the characters are facing. Suggest possible solutions which might be developed; tell why you find these solutions logical.

4. *Just before you read the last chapter:* Have the problems been settled? How? What might the final chapter add to the book? Does it seem that something is still missing?

5. *After you've finished the book:* Make two columns on your paper, headed *Liked* and *Disliked.* List as many things as you can about

your book under each heading. Then, choose one thing you liked and one thing you disliked and explain why.

In my "academic" tracks, where abilities are most heterogeneous, only four out of eighty students failed to complete the five writings. Since there were no "wrong" answers, students felt assured of earning credit in a relatively easy manner; they could try to second-guess the author or just raise questions. It was simple for me to tell not only if students had read their books but also if they had understood what they had read.

I then asked students to do a more formal book report on their chosen novels with written, visual, and oral components. I believe that these products were more detailed and more polished because of the guided freewritings, but I also think this strategy could be used alone effectively to encourage reading and sharing in a more relaxed atmosphere.

Linda S. Slusser, North Ridgeville High School, Ohio

X Marks the Style

An author's writing style is sometimes hard for students to analyze. Before I and my students take a close look at an author's work and writing style, I like to show students how much they can figure out for themselves.

I distribute a handout sheet listing elements of style, in a format similar to that shown below. Next to each element of style is a short line on which students are to position an x. The placement of the x indicates how much or how little the author relies on this element of style.

This list can be used with any work of fiction. Whatever our current reading assignment, I find it much easier to conduct a meaningful discussion on an author's style once students have worked through this exercise.

Place an x on each line to show the author's use of that element of style.

1. Dialogue/no dialogue   D_____ND
2. Emotional/not emotional   E_____NE
3. Humorous/serious   H_____S
4. Slang/no slang   S_____NS
5. Easy vocabulary/difficult
   vocabulary   EV_____DV

6. Figurative language/literal
   language   FL_____LL
7. Easy sentence structure/
   difficult sentence structure   ESS_____DSS
8. Descriptive/not descriptive   D_____ND
9. Realism/fantasy   R_____F

Laurie Barnoski, Tumwater High School, Washington

Literature-Inspired Letter Writing

This is a letter writing assignment for use after teaching "The Rape of the Lock." I'm not sure if it is my own or borrowed, but I do know that it helps my students develop sensitivity to *audience* and *voice*. They also seem to understand the reading more after imagining themselves in the place of the main characters.

After we have read and discussed "The Rape of the Lock," I review the parts of the social letter and the business letter and list on the chalkboard possible audiences for each type of letter. I emphasize the importance of using an appropriate voice for each type of letter. To illustrate differences in tone, I read aloud several sample letters.

Next I ask students to choose one of the assignments listed below. I ask that they use appropriate facts and language to fit the audience and that they carefully proofread their finished letters for correct grammar and punctuation. Students may fabricate names and facts as desired to give more substance to their writing. For an added flair, students may also copy their finished letters on sheets of decorative stationery. I provide pictures of flowery borders used in the eighteenth century for students to imitate in drawing their own.

1. Imagine that you are Belinda and that some time has elapsed since the incident at Hampton Court. Write a friendly (or not-so-friendly) letter to the Baron describing the feelings you now have for him.

2. Imagine that you are the Baron and that some time has elapsed since the incident at Hampton Court. Write a friendly (or not-so-friendly) letter to Belinda describing the feelings you now have for her.

3. Clarissa has opened a counseling service for couples who are having problems in their relationships. Imagine that you are Thalestris and that you would like to apply for a position as counselor. Attach a résumé to your letter.

4. Imagine that you are a lawyer representing either the Baron or Belinda. Write a letter to the other party explaining that your client wishes to bring a lawsuit against him or her. Discuss the reasons for the impending lawsuit and what your client hopes to gain from it.

When the letters are completed, students form groups according to the assignment they have chosen, and read aloud their results. (If one assignment has attracted more than eight or nine students, I ask those students to form two groups instead of one.) Members of each group vote on one letter to be read to the entire class. The rest are displayed on the walls and bulletin boards of our classroom.

Ruth M. Hooks, Northview High School, Dothan, Alabama

Expanding on Wells's *The Time Machine*

Much ado has been made recently in my school system about the value of integrating the various language arts rather than teaching each in isolation. With this in mind, I sought an assignment that would also take into account my not-very-enthusiastic seniors and satisfy the county currriculum requirements that students "write a three- to five-page three-source report and read two novels besides the regular literature assignment."

The research paper has often been a problem for my students, who have a tendency to plagiarize. ("The author said just what I meant in exactly the same words I would have used. . . .") Some students view the whole process as purposeless, "a boring, stupid assignment." Fortunately, the method I have devised motivates students so that they *want* to do the writing themselves. It has proved a winner with students in six different classes.

The assignment is based on H.G. Wells's *The Time Machine.* The first step is for students to read the book. I prefer to have students read and discuss the book by sections in class.

Then I assign the writing of another episode or adventure for the time traveler. In this episode the time traveler must travel into the past from the present day. The student chooses as the traveler's destination any time, place, and event in history. In the student's three- to five-page adventure, the traveler may observe and report the event as a narrator or may become involved in the event; however, he or she may not change the outcome of the event.

I suggest that students choose well-known events so that they are not frustrated in searching for sources. I also suggest that students select events in which they are genuinely interested and that they find ways to incorporate their own hobbies or interests in their writing. A student interested in clothes, for instance, might include elaborate descriptions of the style of dress of the time. A student interested in tools, weapons, transportation, or architecture could focus on those.

Students usually spend three to five days choosing an event and gathering information from books, magazines, and encyclopedias. Students focus on creative writing while at the same time incorporating facts learned in research. And though the end result is closer to historical fiction than to a research paper, each student is required to document his or her research using endnotes and a bibliography, just as with a research paper.

Many of the stories my students wrote last quarter mimicked Wells's writing style and depicted the time traveler in much the same way that Wells did. But Wells could not have imagined the adventures these time travelers had—among them trips to Dallas for Kennedy's assassination; to Pearl Harbor on December 7, 1941; to America with Columbus in 1492; to Vietnam during the conflict involving the United States; and to the moon with astronaut John Glenn.

When the papers are completed, students share them with the class, not by reading, but by telling them as storytellers would.

Mary Latimer, Brookwood High School, Snellville, Georgia

Novel Dialogue

I vary my writing assignments as often as possible to challenge students and keep interest high. In this assignment, students write conversational dialogues based on a story or novel of their choice.

Students first choose out-of-class reading assignments from a list of stories or novels I provide. (The options may be varied according to the interests and abilities of the students.) I set a deadline by which the reading is to be completed. Students are more likely to meet the deadline when they know ahead of time that they will be writing about their books in class on the day of the deadline.

On the writing day, I give students these directions on a handout sheet:

> Write an imaginary dialogue between you and another student about the book you have read. Assume that the other student has not read the book. Your dialogue should include references to the author, plot, setting, characters, and theme, but you don't have to use these exact terms in your dialogue. Also include your

overall impression of the book. The class period will be divided into three parts:

Prewriting (5 minutes): List the questions you think the other student might ask you about your book.

Writing (30 minutes): Write a dialogue based on the questions you listed in prewriting. Both questions and answers should sound normal and conversational, like a casual exchange between two friends. An example follows:

> Me: I just finished a good book. I had to read it for English, but it turned out to be really interesting.
>
> Amy: Yeah? What's it called?
>
> Me: *Huckleberry Finn.*
>
> Amy: Who is it by?
>
> Me: Mark Twain. At least, that's the name he wrote under. His real name was Samuel Langhorne Clemens.

> (From this point, you would continue until you had included all the important information about the book and explained your view of it.)

Rewriting/Revision (5 minutes): You won't have time to write a complete second draft, but in the time left at the end of the class period, you can reread your dialogue and check spelling, punctuation, and usage.

My students say they like trying to write the way they talk. One class period provides just about the right amount of time for writing one dialogue. My students all managed to complete the assignment, and most of the dialogues did sound like two teenagers talking about a book, complete with slang, interruptions for explanations, and even occasional "stupid" questions and sarcastic answers.

Ken Spurlock, Holmes High School, Covington, Kentucky

Hardy's *The Mayor of Casterbridge*

The intricate plot of Thomas Hardy's *The Mayor of Casterbridge* invites a variety of supplementary assignments for in-class or out-of-class work. I have used the following assignments with my seniors with good results.

1. *A comparison-contrast paper:* Students compare and contrast the protagonist, Michael Henchard, to Macbeth, another tragic hero whom they have studied. I introduce students to the term *hubris* and emphasize its importance in bringing about the downfall of the protagonist. Optionally, this paper can be developed into a research paper.

2. *Two letter-writing assignments: A.* Students each put on the persona of either Henchard or Farfrae and write a business letter that could have been written during the course of the novel— such as a letter from Farfrae to the mayor of Dover concerning the festivities soon to take place upon arrival of the dignitary. *B.* Male students write a love letter to Lucetta, pretending they are Henchard. Female students each answer one of these letters, using an appropriately loving tone. The letters are checked for proper form and, amid much laughter, read aloud.

3. *Résumé:* Students write a résumé that would help Henchard find a position after he loses everything.

4. *Obituary and epitaph:* Students research the proper format for obituaries and epitaphs and write one of each for the protagonist. I find this a good time to acquaint students with the meanings of the terms *bathos* and *pathos.*

5. *Invitation and acceptance:* I explain the meaning and purpose of R.S.V.P. Students fold paper to make cards and write wedding invitations and acceptances for the Donald Farfrae-Elizabeth Jane wedding and reception.

6. *Role-playing:* With help from the entire class, I stage a mock trial of the Furmity woman, Henchard presiding. Ironically, this generally turns out to be Henchard's trial, not the Furmity woman's.

7. *Booklist with annotated bibliography:* Now is the time for students to brush up on research skills. Elizabeth Jane loves books; students research popular books of the era and list titles they think she would have read for self-improvement. The bibliography is good practice for the college prep student.

8. *Matching a character from the book with a character from a TV program:* This gets students thinking about characterization. For example, my students compare Lucetta with a lurid lover from the "soaps." The frustrated, Machiavellian "Henchard type" also can be found in many television programs.

9. *Display of musical talent (strictly optional):* A willing and able music student can sometimes be persuaded to learn a Scottish ballad and sing it to the class, imitating Farfrae.

Kay McCrory, Portland High School, Tennessee

Poetry à la Emily Dickinson

Ask students to read Emily Dickinson's poem "Fame."

> Fame is a bee.
>   It has a song —
> It has a sting —
>   Ah, too, it has a wing.

You may wish to discuss concepts such as figurative language, metaphorical expression, symbolism, abstract nouns, and literary theme prior to reading or to wait until students have read and responded to the poem.

When students have read the poem and had a few moments to reflect, ask, "What do you think Emily Dickinson is trying to say to her readers?" Ask students, too, how they would interpret fame's "song," fame's "sting," and fame's "wing."

Following discussion of the poem's language and theme, tell students that they will be writing poems in the same format as Dickinson's "Fame." Help students brainstorm nouns for abstract concepts, such as *anger, imagination, power, wealth,* and so on. Record suggestions on the chalkboard or on chart paper.

At this point, each student chooses one noun from the list and makes a list of words and phrases that describe it. For example, the noun *anger* might elicit these words and phrases: "destructive," "raging," "can't be bottled up." Then students select an animal possessing some of the same qualities, such as a tiger for anger. In a second list, students list qualities or attributes of the animal, such as "sharp claws," "a fast runner," "fierce," "takes its prey by surprise," "protects its young," and so on.

As they begin to write, students must decide which of the possible comparisons between the abstract concept and the animal will make the best poem, and which comparison might provide the "twist" for the last line. For instance, a student comparing anger to a tiger could try to imagine anger, in turn, having "sharp claws," being "a fast runner," being "fierce," "taking its prey by surprise," and "protecting its young." In this example, a possible last line might be created by changing "protecting its young" to "it protects its own." Suggest that students experiment until they find a comparison for the last line that, like Dickinson's, causes the reader to stop and think.

Students follow the format below in writing their poems. Note that they may substitute *is* or another verb for *has*.

      _____ is a _____.
        It has a _____ —
    It has a _____ —
        Ah, too, it has a _____.

Here's an example written by one of my students:

    Love is a mole.
      It can be secretive —
    It can build tunnels —
      Ah, too, it can be blind.
        Masahiro Masamoto

I have found that far from being limiting, the requirements imposed by this format can produce striking and highly original metaphors.

Students illustrate, combine, and bind their finished poems into a classroom poetry anthology. As a follow-up to this exercise, make available copies of other poems by Emily Dickinson as well as other poems that illustrate the use of symbolism.

Sarah Sherman-Siegel, Kew-Forest School, Forest Hills, New York

Poetry Image Collage

In teaching a poetry unit, the image collage can be an effective tool to help reduce the anxiety with which students often approach poetry and to help students think about the images that poems create. The materials needed for this activity include paper, scissors, glue, and a supply of newspapers and magazines. The time required is two class periods.

I use this activity after class discussion of essential elements of poetry, such as imagery, rhythm, tone, and rhyme. I place the necessary materials on a side table and give students a choice of poems from which to create their image collages.

Instructions are simple. Each student is to study the chosen poem and create a collage representing the image or images that he or she sees in the poem, using pictures and parts of pictures cut out from magazines and newspapers. I ask students to have definite ideas of the images their poems create before beginning to arrange their collages. The goal is not merely to create a picture of people or places suggested in the poem, but to re-create the poem's mood and impact. The most creative arrangements may even be able to suggest the rhythm, tone, and rhyme of the poems that inspired them.

When my students are finished, I line their collages up on the chalk tray and let the class try to guess which poem inspired each collage. As part of our discussion, students are to explain what they had in mind in creating their collages and answer classmates' questions about specific parts of the arrangement as they relate to the poem. This leads into discussion of the images used in the poems, the imaginative ways in which students conveyed these images, and, additionally, the different interpretations students sometimes had of the same poem.

Melinda Derrick, Gatlinburg, Tennessee

A *Foxfire* Introduction to *The Grapes of Wrath*

My students don't know much about the Depression, nor do many of them have more than limited firsthand knowledge of the extended family. To prepare students for our reading of *The Grapes of Wrath,* I ask them to complete the following assignment inspired by the *Foxfire* books.

I ask students to interview someone who lived through the Depression and to record not only short-answer responses but stories and reminiscences that arise spontaneously during the interview. I provide one or two class periods for students to work in small groups generating interview questions. I give this assignment about a week before spring break because I know some of my students visit aunts, uncles, grandparents, or other older relatives during the break. Students may also choose to interview neighbors or friends of their parents, and are free to enlist help in finding a suitable person to interview.

Students come back from spring break with the results of their interviews in final form. I schedule one or two class periods for us to talk about what they learned and what surprised them most in the stories they heard. I then make multiple photocopies of the final copies so that each student has a booklet of Depression recollections to read before we begin *The Grapes of Wrath*.

Ellen Geisler, Mentor High School, Madison, Ohio

Literary T-Shirts

When my advanced senior English classes study Shakespeare, I require that students design a T-shirt or sweatshirt with a Shakespeare quotation written on the front and what I term a "Shake-scene" drawn on the back. A "Shake-scene" is a depiction of something relating to Shakespeare's life or work—a scene from a play, a drawing of a prop such as a skull or a sword, or a depiction directly inspired by the chosen

quotation. I give students plenty of advance warning for this assignment, and the results range from humorous to impressive. The T-shirt produced by one student almost brought tears to my eyes. On the front he had printed in bright colors these lines from *Julius Caesar:* "Cowards die many times before their deaths;/ The valiant never taste of death but once." On the back he had drawn the *Challenger* space shuttle.

My own T-shirt bears these words from *Macbeth:* "Double, double, toil and trouble," along with a picture of a witch on the back. Students tell me the shirt is appropriate, but they smile when they say it.

Kay McCrory, Portland High School, Tennessee

Remembering Pearl Harbor

For several years I had a gnawing uneasiness about students' lack of general knowledge of important places and events, aggravated when I asked every December about Pearl Harbor and received only blank stares. Feeling the need to expose students to more nonfiction and desiring more opportunities for interdisciplinary approaches, our team prepared a World War II unit for seventh- or eighth-grade English language arts classes. I have used this unit again in succeeding years with only minor changes and have found that it helped students understand the causes and results of past wars as well as the general effects of war on young and old everywhere. To anyone preparing a unit on this topic I would also recommend a recent *ALAN Review* (Winter 1986) containing an excellent article entitled "World War II and Its Relevance to Today's Adolescents."

The unit as outlined here can be accomplished in three or four weeks, though adding or subtracting readings and activities could easily expand or condense its focus. We began just after Thanksgiving by reading Walter Lord's thoroughly researched *Day of Infamy.* (This is best read in its entirety, but major portions, carefully selected, can be used if time is a problem.)

We then spent a few days with a recording of FDR's "Day of Infamy" speech (available on the Audio Archives label or the Visual Education Corporation label) and a CBS script of "The Waltons—Day of Infamy," both excellent complementary resources. Students and teachers looked in attics and costume shops for clothes from the '40s to wear on December 7, and others retold stories their grandparents had shared about December 1941 and the war years. Our readings, activities, and daily attention to maps of the Pacific all helped students understand the retrospective commentary offered by newspapers, television, and radio on December 7.

As I and my co-workers assigned further readings, we recognized that most students had read parts or all of *The Diary of Anne Frank,* and so we chose books to build on students' background knowledge: *Night* by Elie Weisel and *The Upstairs Room* by Johanna Reiss. These books not only gave students a deeper appreciation for Anne Frank's

Diary but presented a vivid picture of how World War II affected the daily life of thousands.

Other reading materials I would recommend are Monica Sone's book *Nisei Daughter* and Jeanne Wakatsuki Houston's and James D. Houston's more recent *Farewell to Manzanar,* accounts of Japanese families living in California at the time of the attack on Pearl Harbor. These are particularly interesting in light of recent revelations about U.S. internment camps for Japanese Americans. Time permitting, a few days might also be spent in the exploration and discussion of Japanese and European cultures and customs.

Because of nautical and military terms in some of the readings, teachers may want to provide vocabulary guides or glossing sheets and to make frequent checks for understanding. Writing assignments such as the following can enhance reading and discussion throughout the unit:

> first-person narratives about surviving an attack
>
> newspaper editorials from the point of view of someone living at the time
>
> impressions of events from a reporter's point of view
>
> journal entries
>
> letter writing

At the close of the unit, student volunteers may spend two or three days presenting accounts of interviews they conducted with relatives or other persons who survived WW II.

My coworkers and I felt that students grew in many ways in pursuing this unit on World War II. The topic afforded exceptional opportunities for promoting language skills as well as a deeper understanding of a significant historical event.

Lanny Van Allen, Austin, Texas

"The Best Book I Have Ever Read . . ."

The idea of assigning book talks as opposed to book reports has appealed to me ever since I discovered that my students had become experts at copying the text from jacket book flaps and calling it their own. However, until I used this assignment, I never imagined the extent to which book talks could motivate outside reading.

I compile a list of classic and adolescent novels and ask each student to choose one for outside reading. After reading, students prepare informal book talks and present them for the students in a general-level English class.

I tell my students that the most important goal for this book-talk assignment is to make listeners curious enough to read the book themselves. Instead of concentrating on biographical facts and on plot descriptions, students focus attention on why they enjoyed or didn't enjoy the novel, what they learned from the novel, and what they learned from reading about the author.

To help students avoid the trite beginning "This novel is about . . .," I suggest that a book talk begin with an anecdote related to the novel or the author. This might be a retelling of the student's favorite part of the story or a description of an incident from the author's life. Most importantly, it should be something that catches the attention of the listeners. Students may still include biographical facts about the author and descriptions of characters, settings, and plot, but this type of information is kept brief.

I also ask students to incorporate in their book talks short answers to the following questions:

1. What qualifies the author to write this book?
2. What is the goal of the author in writing this book?
3. What did you find most interesting as you read this book?
4. What is the most interesting thing you learned about the author?

I warn students not to give away the whole plot of the book; listeners should be left with a sense of suspense.

The best thing about this activity is the fact that it gets both presenters and listeners interested in reading the novels on the list.

Dana S. Witwer, River Valley High School, Marion, Ohio

Animal Magnetism

I have a very personal tactic for motivating students to use detail in writing: I bring to class my ancient stuffed animals to be subjects for our writing exercise. Part of this idea's success probably stems from the fact that each of these bedraggled stuffed animals conveys a distinct sense of personality that students enjoy bringing out in their writings.

At the beginning of the class period, students form groups of two or three. A student from each group draws the name of one of the animals from a grab bag, after which I introduce the animals to the appropriate groups. (The more ragged the animal, the more students seem to like it.) The members of the group then work together to write a one- or two-paragraph description of their stuffed animal.

I emphasize that the goal is not to produce a string of details but to create a strong, vivid impression of the "personality" of the stuffed animal. This requires that students, once in their groups, consider and discuss the impression they want to create in their descriptions, the details to include, and the specific words that best convey the desired effect. After rough drafts are exchanged within groups for feedback, students revise their writings and read them aloud to the class.

Initially a few students scoff at my menagerie, but eventually most students get into the spirit of discussion and description. More than once I have received an offer to buy one of the animals from my collection—offers which I, of course, declined. I have learned to expect references later in the semester to "Freckles the Dog" and "Praetorian Bear."

Judith Erickson Surovek, Griffith Senior High School, Indiana

Using Pictures to Teach Poetry

Students often complain to me that they don't like poetry because they can't understand it. I recently thought of a way to help students more readily "clue in" to the subjects and emotions described in poems. As I am reading through the dozen or so magazines to which I subscribe, I often cut out pictures of interesting, dramatic, or unusual people, scenes, or landscapes as inspiration for my own writing and painting. I realized that the same pictures and photographs that evoked strong feelings in me would probably evoke strong feelings in my students, and thus help them understand the inspiration for and development of a poem. In addition, the cutout pictures provide a handy reference in the discusson and use of figurative language and figures of speech.

I begin by passing a picture around the class, asking students to describe both the picture and the feelings it evokes. To develop thinking skills, I follow up questions with additional questions along the same lines, rather than supplying students with answers.

Sometimes I use a photograph clipped from a newsmagazine, showing the anguished face of an elderly Greek woman. I ask students:

> What is this woman's state of mind?
>
> Why do you think she is upset?
>
> How do you feel about her while looking at the picture?
>
> What words and phrases best describe her?
>
> If you were trying to describe this picture to someone who had not seen it, to what would you compare her actions and expression?

I list students' short answers on the chalkboard. Whenever possible, I use gentle probing to encourage students to use metaphors and similes in their answers. For instance, I might refer to an aerial view of a town and ask students, "Do the tiny human figures in this picture remind you of anything?" Holding up a picture of an elephant, I might ask, "What other huge objects does this elephant make you think of?" Following our discussion, each student receives a picture cut out of a magazine and responds to it in the same way we did as a group. Students examine the pictures carefully and either write out their responses or present them orally to the rest of the class.

Next, I introduce a poem that has a theme similar to that of the picture we discussed together in class. For instance, to accompany the photograph of the anguished woman, I might choose a poem about war, the death of a loved one, or divorce. I prompt students to compare the poem and the picture by asking such questions as:

> What similarities are there between the picture and the poem?
>
> How are the moods of the picture and poem different?
>
> Could the woman in the picture be feeling the same feelings as are described or suggested in the poem?
>
> Does hearing the poem give you more ideas on what this woman could be thinking?
>
> Does seeing this woman's face make it easier for you to relate to the theme of the poem?

As the final stage of this activity, I ask students to write poems, stories, or one-act plays using their pictures as inspiration. Most students seem to have ideas already, due to the talking and writing they have done about their pictures.

Grace Cooper, Hyattsville, Maryland

Exploring Conflict

Before my students read a selection involving parent-child conflict (the selection is determined by interests and availability of materials and thus may change from year to year), I prepare them by distributing a short handout containing a synopsis of a scene from the film *Rebel without a Cause* (Warner Brothers, 1955). We briefly discuss the nature of the scene and I relate it to the plot of the film as a whole. (This activity could be based just as easily on a scene of parent-child conflict from another film, play, or novel, such as Steinbeck's *East of Eden*, Williams's *The Glass Menagerie*, or Greene's *The Summer of My German Soldier*.

Next I play a Warner Brothers Records recording of the scene in which Jim (James Dean) returns home late at night after being involved in a hot-rod race that killed another teenager. He is confronted by his parents (Jim Backus and Ann Doran), who seem as confused as he is. Jim's mother is particularly critical of him. During the argument, Jim accuses his father of being cowardly and begs him, "Dad, stand up for me!" Tension develops rapidly. Finally, Jim flies into a rage and physically attacks his father. Brief though this scene is, the performances carry tremendous emotional impact.

After students have listened to the recording, I ask them a number of questions, starting with a focus on literal comprehension and moving to evaluation. I ask such questions as:

> What kind of trouble was Jim in?
>
> What caused the argument?
>
> How did Jim's father react to him?
>
> How did Jim's mother's reactions differ from those of his father?
>
> Why did Jim accuse his father of being weak?
>
> Should Jim have gone to the police with the truth? Why or why not?
>
> What do you think Jim meant when he said, "It doesn't matter, Mother, it doesn't matter, it doesn't matter!"?
>
> How did you feel when Jim attacked his father? Could you predict that this would happen? If so, what clues helped you?
>
> What would you have done if you had been in Jim's predicament? (You may answer in terms of the accident *and* the family argument.)
>
> Which character seems most deserving of sympathy? Explain.

Depending on the class, I may ask students to write their answers before discussion begins or begin discussion immediately after the recording ends.

Following discussion, students are instructed to write a one-paragraph "reaction paper" expressing some of their feelings about the scene. For example, one of my students who had seen the movie wrote on why Jim was perceived as a "rebel without a cause." Other topics students might want to touch on include:

> what Jim could have done differently
>
> how the parents *should* have reacted
>
> how the scene might have been different if written from the viewpoint of the mother or father
>
> how the family situation made this argument "inevitable"

the different ways that this scene could be followed up in the movie

I have found this activity worthwhile in several ways. First, it helps students make conscious connections between reading (handout) and listening (recording), thereby sharpening comprehension. Secondly, it helps students see relationships between literary works (the scene from *Rebel without a Cause* and the subsequent reading assignment). Thirdly, it develops thinking skills by requiring that students analyze the characters' behavior, support particular points of view, and project themselves into hypothetical situations. In addition, this activity "primes the pump" for discussions about interpersonal problems in stories, plays, poems, and novels studied later.

Larry Crapse, Florence School District One, South Carolina

Tell Me Yours and I'll Tell You Mine

When teaching short stories, I sometimes ask students to write diary entries or short narratives from the point of view of different characters in the story. The benefits of this strategy come when students separate into groups of four or five, read their accounts aloud, and compare and contrast their depictions of characters and motivations. Students' different responses promote lively discussion of the author's treatment of character. In trying to justify their opinions with passages from the text, students also further their understanding of the story.

This exercise has worked particulary well with de Maupassant's "The Necklace" and Shirley Jackson's "The Lottery." For the former, I ask students to write Mathilde Loisel's diary entry for the night she learns the truth about the necklace; students have responded with entries ranging from suicidal intentions to divorce to recovering the real jewels and proposing a happy ending after all. For "The Lottery," I ask students to write an account of the events as told by a member of Tessie Hutchinson's family, again with widely varying results. As another of its benefits, this exercise also helps students understand the difference between first-person and third-person narration.

Helen Jaskoski, Fullerton, California

3 Prewriting and Writing

Whatever we conceive well, we express clearly.

Nicolas Boileau

The writing activities in this section are intended to help students accomplish both these aims—conceiving well and expressing clearly. Among the tasks students will tackle are writing an operating manual for a common household device, analyzing the interactions of writing response groups, practicing the writing of descriptive detail, and writing the most trite, clichéd story possible.

An Operating Manual for the Safety Pin

There is little writing more attractive to my students than the operating manual for a new car. Seeing students poring over a few such manuals, I decided to have them try their hands at writing their own "how-to" manuals. This assignment helps students organize their thoughts and write clearly, as well as stimulating creativity.

I ask students to bring to class manuals or operating instruction booklets for common household devices. We discuss the types of information likely to be found in one of these manuals, such as:

a catchy slogan

an attractive cover picture

a description of parts

a breakdown of function and explanation of each part

warnings regarding safety precautions

The writing assignment is to take a simple object—safety pin, pencil, stapler, headphone set—and write a short technical manual, complete with illustrations, explaining the object's design, function, and operation. I find that different students take different approaches. Some organize their manual according to functions, placing the most important function first. Others divide the manual into three sections:

functions, use, and care. Whatever means of organization they use, students discover immediately that they need to write carefully and exactly, using specific details. Any vague or inaccurate references are pointed out when we read aloud and discuss the finished results.

Other variations on this idea might include asking students to write a technical manual for a human being, or asking each student to write a more thorough manual for some more complicated device with which he or she is familiar.

Fred Mednick, Oakwood School, North Hollywood, California

Fishbowl Feedback

This idea isn't new, but it's worth using for the insight it gives students into the interactions of writing response groups. The activity involves a student demonstration group and a fishbowl seating arrangement— a circle of chairs facing inward surrounded by chairs for observers.

Before rearranging the chairs, I talk to students about the different ways they can help each other in their writing response groups. For example, I advise students to be more specific about what they like and what confuses them. I also suggest that whenever they criticize some aspect of another student's writing, they offer concrete suggestions for how to improve the problem area. I briefly explain some of the ways in which feedback can help writers develop, and I urge students to support one another in the early stages of composing.

Next, we arrange five chairs in a circle in the center of the room. I ask for five volunteers to role-play the members of a writing response group. The rest of the students seat themselves around the fishbowl, where they can observe the group's interactions.

One of the five volunteers plays the writer and reads aloud an actual draft of a writing in progress. Before reading, he or she explains what stage the writing is in (brainstorming, early draft, later draft) and what kind of help he or she needs ("I need some ideas on where the plot should go from here," "I need help making the dialogues more realistic"). While the writer reads, the other group members listen and take notes. Afterward they discuss the writing, describe their reactions, and give the writer feedback.

When everyone in the group has had a chance to contribute something to the discussion, I ask the class, including the demonstrators, to do a short freewriting on the group interaction. I ask students to consider whether the writer was specific enough in asking for feedback, which of the group's comments seemed most helpful, what problems they observed, what suggestions they would make for improving group interaction, and so on.

Finally, I ask a few volunteers to read their freewritings aloud, which typically evolves into a full-class discussion on writing groups. As students offer comments, I record their suggestions on the board. By the end of the discussion we have a list of helpful guidelines for effective group work, which I type up and photocopy for my students.

Mike Steinberg, Michigan State University, East Lansing, Michigan

She Shows Sea Slides of the Seashore

I have finally discovered a use for the yellow boxes of slides piled high in the corner of my sewing room. I search out my most inspiring slides of mountains, deserts, and foreign lands and take them to school, where I add them to prepared slides from the library and slides I have created in the Service Center. The ultimate destination for all these slides is the famous slide show in Room 108. I use these spectacular and unusual scenes to draw out my students' powers of creative description and to spice up writing practice of topic sentences and supporting sentences. Here are the steps I use when I present the slide show:

1. Upon first seeing the slide, each student writes down a descriptive word or phrase that captures an initial impression.

2. Students list specific details to support their first impressions.

3. After students have seen all the slides and responded, I run through the slides again. We share impressions of the scenes and choose favorites.

4. Students write paragraphs on their favorite scenes, using the first impression as the topic sentence and the supporting details in following sentences.

Participation is high in this activity, as students search for the best word to describe each scene and then compete to create the most vivid description. Students are always curious about where and when each slide was taken; when I go back through the slides a second time I include a few more details about the ones I took myself. This exercise is also useful when I can dig up slides of Roman ruins or the gardens behind Shakespeare's home and thus pique student interest in future reading assignments.

Leslie Johnson, Westwood High School, Austin, Texas

Contest for the Worst Story

Teaching short story writing to high school students is always a difficult task; often the biggest obstacle to overcome is student resistance. After facing moaning and groaning students for several years, I finally hit upon a way to interest students in writing short stories and, at the same time, to open students' eyes to the pitfalls of stock situations, trite characters, and clichés in dialogue: I sponsored a "Worst Short Story Contest" for my twelfth-grade composition class.

I asked students to write the most trite, clichéd short stories they could produce, and the results were both hilarious and effective. It was amazing how many stock lines and characters my twelfth graders came up with. Phrases such as "little did they know" and "suddenly a shot rang out" were abundant. But what the students found most amusing was how many of the stories, although written individually, ended up being basically the same story—"girl sighs after boy; boy doesn't know girl exists; freak accident; eyes meet." You know the story. So did they.

After we read the stories aloud in class, students voted for the "Worst Short Story." I followed this assignment by asking students to write "real" short stories, explaining that the previous attempt should have been a cathartic experience, freeing their minds from trite phrases, characters, and situations. Judging from the results, my claim turned out to have some substance.

Erin W. Duffy, Wakefield School, Huntley, Virginia

Pet Rock Reports

This activity provides students practice in descriptive technique and characterization. My sophomores enjoy it a great deal; I'm sure it would be popular with other levels as well. I got the idea from the Pet Rock craze several years ago.

Students are to bring a rock to class the day of the exercise. To avoid finding any boulders in the classroom, I stipulate that the rock should fit easily in the student's hand. I bring a few extras for students who forget theirs.

I tell students that they will need a lot of imagination for this exercise, enough, in fact, to make their rocks "come to life." I explain that I will ask a series of questions to help the class get to know their rocks better. Students make up responses and jot them down. Responses should be as specific as possible, since they will be used by other students to identify the rocks later in the class period. These are the questions I ask:

1. What is your rock's name?
2. How is your rock colored?
3. What is the texture of your rock?
4. What are the approximate dimensions of your rock?
5. What is the shape of your rock? What, if anything, does its shape remind you of?
6. What interesting experiences has your rock had?
7. Describe that special moment when you and your rock first met.
8. What do you think the future holds for your rock?

When students finish answering the last question, I collect responses and rocks. I distribute the responses among students, making sure that no student gets his or her own sheet. As students read the response sheets, they should note especially the description of the rock. Then I place all the rocks (along with a few decoys) on a table and let students take turns selecting the rock that matches the description. Students who become frustrated trying to find a particular rock are asked to comment on what additional information on color, shape, texture, and dimensions might have helped to find the rock more quickly.

After each student has selected a rock, it's time for a reunion. Holding a response sheet and the rock that supposedly corresponds to it, I call out the name of the rock. The owner of the rock either claims the rock or, if it is not the correct rock, goes looking through the rock collection for the right rock. Eventually, after much trading and examining of rocks, all the rocks are reunited with their rightful owners.

I often use this activity as a preface to discussing descriptive technique in general. I also like to bring up the importance of detailed character development. I point out that many authors have created a past for characters (much like the pasts students created for their rocks) and that even if the character's past is not described in the story or novel, the character is likely to be more fully developed as a result of the author's thorough preparation.

Finally, we hold a ceremony for those rocks whose owners are putting their rocks out to pasture, and dump the unlucky rocks outside my window for next year's sophomores to adopt.

Russell Barrett, Cooper High School, Abilene, Texas

Tackling the College Application Essay

Some of the most thought-provoking essay topics in my repertoire are those I've adapted from actual college application forms. Below are the instructions I give for an in-class essay-writing assignment:

College application forms often ask you to write an essay. Following are some essay questions taken from some of these forms. Read them all carefully, and then pick *one* of the questions and answer it as if you were seeking acceptance to that college. Don't ask how long your response should be; just write a good essay.

1. The Committee on Admissions would like to know as much about each individual candidate as possible. Please write a short essay telling us what *you* think we ought to know about you to make the best possible decision on your application to this university.

2. If you were to write a book, what theme or subject matter would it be based on and why?

3. What is the worst thing that ever happened to you and how did you cope with it?

4. Write a short autobiographical sketch that focuses upon an experience or event of unusual significance to you.

5. Write a short essay about a recent and significant action of yours and its consequences for you or others.

6. This university believes that the aims of a liberal arts education are best attained with a heterogeneous community and thus encourages applications from members of all cultural, racial, religious, and socioeconomic groups. If, in light of this statement, you would like us to consider information about your own background or the background of your parents, please specify.

7. Discuss some issue of personal, local, or national concern and its importance to you.

8. Indicate a person who has had a significant influence on you, and describe that influence.

9. If you could spend the evening with one of the following people, whom would you choose? Indira Gandhi, Alfred Hitchcock, Ronald Reagan, Coretta Scott King, Elvis Presley, Luciano Pavarotti, (your choice). Why? What would you talk about?

10. If you were given the opportunity to leave a time capsule for posterity in the cornerstone of your city hall, what one book, one mechanical object, and one other item of your own choosing would you leave as a statement about life in the late twentieth century? Explain your choices.

Curt Crotty, Evanston Township High School, Illinois

Senior Scrapbook

For years my younger sister kept a piece of bubblegum on her crowded bulletin board as a reminder of a date with the boy who later became her husband. Recently, that treasured and preserved bubblegum gave me the idea for a writing project that has become very popular with seniors.

In this assignment, seniors start a scrapbook at the beginning of the school year. Throughout the year students collect items that, though perhaps insignificant to others, hold special memories of significant events. Students have complete freedom in selecting items for inclusion in their scrapbooks, as well as in creating themes and covers. The one requirement is that students write a paragraph or two about each item included in their scrapbooks, recording the sights, sounds, smells, tastes, thoughts, and feelings surrounding the event. I set aside a class period every so often for students to draft and polish entries for their scrapbooks. However, the majority of the writing is done outside class over the course of the year.

What began small has since ballooned into a project that seniors look forward to and participate in eagerly. My senior students can be heard talking about their scrapbooks at football games, dances, parties, and in the school halls as they look for different and original items to collect. Among the mementos that have made their way into students' scrapbooks are photographs, a popcorn box, a speeding ticket, a chin strap, a plastic bag full of mud, and shrimp from a homecoming dinner. I have yet to hear anyone complain about the writing required for this project. Students realize that when their senior year is over, they'll be glad to have a record of adventures and mishaps to help them reminisce.

Lori Ables, Pleasant Grove High School, Texarkana, Texas

A Noteworthy Assignment

For a change of pace, give students an assignment in notewriting. Notewriting may sound utilitarian and dull, but in this assignment it calls for clear thinking, an awareness of audience, and creativity, as students are challenged to pack the necessary details into as few words as possible. Here are students' instructions and writing topics in handout form:

> *Instructions:* Fold a sheet of blank typing paper into fourths and open it back up. Notice that the folds create four equal blocks. Your assignment is to choose four options from the list below and write four corresponding notes, one in each of the four blocks.

Since you don't have a lot of room to write, you will need to be as concise as possible. At the same time, you will need to add some specifics to each note. For instance, in the first note, a few well-chosen words would be enough to explain what you borrowed, from whom you borrowed it, why you borrowed it, and how you plan to show your appreciation to the item's owner.

Vary each note's tone to fit the intended recipient. A note to a friend should sound more personal and familiar than a note to Mrs. Johnson at the dry cleaner's. Include the date, a salutation, and an appropriate closing in each note.

1. While your brother or sister was away, you borrowed something very important to him or her. Write a note to your brother or sister explaining what you did and apologizing for borrowing the item without asking.

2. You will be out of town for a week with your family. Write a note to one of your teachers asking about the work you will miss.

3. You made an awful stain on your white wool sweater. Write a note to the employees at the dry cleaner's explaining what the stain is and why you need the sweater back right away.

4. You have exciting news for your best friend. Write a note to him or her setting up a time to talk.

5. You were given a detention. Write a note to someone at home explaining that you won't be free after school to run the errand you had promised to take care of.

6. You lost money in a vending machine. Write a note to the next person who will use the machine.

7. You are going to a meeting at the school Tuesday evening and don't have a ride home. Write a note to a student who lives near you but whom you don't know well, requesting a ride home after the meeting.

8. A relative called to say that he or she is going to be passing through in the next day or two and plans to stop for a visit. Write a note to your mom or dad about the call.

Marilyn McGivney, Walnut Creek, California

Keeping Research Under Control

Occasionally I give students a break from the difficulties of selecting topics and finding sources and myself a break from running to the library to check for plagiarism. I accomplish this by assigning a "controlled research paper."

In using this assignment, I set a general topic and provide enough resources so that each student can focus on a different aspect of the topic. For instance, if I choose *alcoholism* as the topic, I run ten copies each of various articles about alcoholism. I might provide as many as twenty-five folders in the resource center, each containing ten copies of one article from a newspaper, magazine, pamphlet, or encyclopedia. On the front of each folder, I attach a library checkout card. After students select thesis statements, they look through these folders and check out copies of articles overnight to make their note cards and bibliography cards.

Except for choosing their own topics, students still have all of the usual research paper tasks—taking notes, making footnotes, organizing materials, writing drafts, and setting up a bibliography from a variety of sources. No two finished papers are ever alike, but since all the papers share a common general topic, they lend themselves to comparison and contrast. A class discussion of the finished results can highlight the different ways in which members of the class approached the assignment and can help students see the strengths and weaknesses of their papers.

Do I get tired of reading forty papers on alcoholism? Of course. But when I find myself efficiently checking students' sources against the articles in the folders, rather than making a dozen trips to the library, I feel grateful for an occasional break from the traditional research paper.

JoAnne Ellis, Cassville High School, Missouri

Theme Papers Revisited

Many of us spend hours marking content and grammatical errors in themes before we return them, only to have students give a perfunctory glance, stash the themes away, and make the same mistakes in the next writing assignment. I use a "theme analysis sheet" to prompt students to look carefully at their last themes before beginning the next ones. In completing these analysis sheets, students learn to correct past errors, to set goals for writing and editing, and to see writing improvement as a cumulative process. In between writing assignments, each student completes a theme analysis sheet and staples it to the top page of his or her last theme paper.

The content of my theme analysis sheet is shown below in condensed form.

Part One: Looking Back

1. Title and subject of your last theme:
2. Major content problem:
3. Major organizational problem:
4. Two grammatical errors:

Part Two: Looking Ahead

1. Title and subject of current theme:
2. Goals for the content of this paper:
3. Goals for the organization of this paper:
4. Goals for improving grammar usage in this paper:

Part Three: Self-Analysis

What I intend to do differently in writing this theme to make it better than the last theme:

Lynn P. Dieter, Maine East High School, Park Ridge, Illinois

Student Magazines

I use this writing project at the freshman level in college, but with minor changes it should work at almost any level. The idea began several years back when, dissatisfied with available anthologies, I decided to try using current general-interest magazines as a source for readings in my expository writing classes. I thought it would help motivate my students to be using "real" writings about the "real" world.

The readings worked out well, but then I got to thinking about the writing segment of the course. Believing in the value of modeling, I decided that if students were *reading* magazines, they probably ought to be *writing* them as well. And that's exactly what I had students do.

I divided the class into groups of five or six students each and assigned each group the task of producing a single complete magazine by semester's end. For each group magazine, the students themselves selected the theme (sports, current events, the arts, health, computers, and so on), the page format, and the staffing.

Every student was given responsibility for coordinating one or more aspects of the finished product. For example, one student might be assigned as overall art director and as editor of the "Letters to the Editor" section. Collectively, the group as a whole served both as production team and as editorial review board.

Besides filling supervisory roles, all students in a group were responsible for providing text and artwork for the various sections of the magazine. By the end of the semester, a student working on a women's fashion and health magazine might have written the following:

a letter to the editor

an article on trends in swimwear

a question and answer column

an advertisement for a new brand of vitamins

a recommendation for an aerobic exercise program

a classified ad

a product review

A student working on a magazine about the arts might contribute such items as:

a letter to the editor

a cartoon

a review of a play opening on Broadway

an interview with a fictitious dancer

a short story

an announcement of an art show opening

an advertisement for a book about the Impressionist painters

Students kept cumulative folders of their writings so that I could review and evaluate their efforts periodically.

Students continued to examine and use as models the current issues of magazines in our classroom. Week by week their own magazines were developed through group meetings and individual work. I was a roving resource person, and also offered instruction in the form of workshops on the different modes of composing required for different sections of the magazines. Among other things, I advised students on the format for editors' responses in the "Letters to the Editor" section; the informal tone appropriate for question-and-answer columns; the formal, objective tone used in news analyses; the style of advertising language; the appropriate tone and content for reviews of products, books, or performances; and the types of questions usually asked in interviews.

Preparing magazines provided an ideal context for peer tutoring, since the writers and reviewers were equally motivated to produce the best material possible. The editorial committee for each magazine reviewed all materials as they were submitted and made suggestions to help writers improve their submissions. As the text and artwork reached the final stages, members of the group worked together in planning and executing the layout of each section, preparing a table of contents, providing section titles, numbering the pages, and devising a cover.

This project was most satisfying for my students when they were allowed to "publish" multiple copies of their completed magazines. One option might be to photocopy a master copy of each magazine, but the method used for reproduction is irrelevant as long as the results are as attractive and professional as local budgets and facilities will permit.

Several additional benefits have accrued from the decision to prepare and "publish" our class magazines as professionally as possible. By showing the results to parents and administrators, I was able to get increased support for this and similar projects. By showing the previous year's efforts to an incoming class, I could more easily motivate them to similar achievements. And finally, I now have souvenirs to help me remember the good times I shared with students from years past.

Wayne Dickson, Stetson University, DeLand, Florida

Support Your Local Topic Sentence

One of the most difficult concepts to teach an unmotivated student with poor verbal skills is the use of specific details to support topic sentences. To motivate such students and to provide the basis for writing practice, I enlisted the aid of our local car dealerships. Several cooperative salespeople provided me with multiple copies of descriptive sales brochures for the latest models of their automobiles and trucks. Armed with over one hundred brochures, I asked students to browse through the collection and to select the automobile they would most like to own. Students eagerly perused the material and each made a decision, keeping the brochure that described his or her final choice.

Next we reviewed the basics of paragraph writing. I read aloud examples from several brochures to illustrate topic sentences, logical organization within paragraphs, and descriptive details backing up topic sentences. The short, simple paragraphs used in the brochures made it easier for students to follow a discussion of these concepts and to examine the organization of the paragraphs. After some discussion, I asked students to skim through their brochures and find examples of descriptive details backing up topic sentences. They read aloud the examples, identifying first the topic sentence and then the related details.

Finally, I asked students to practice using supporting details by writing, in their own words, descriptions of the cars they had chosen. I asked them to check to see that each paragraph made a clear statement and then backed it up. As an example, I told students that if a topic sentence claimed that a particular car was the fastest on the road, I would expect the sentences that followed to provide proof with concrete details such as "a powerful engine," "an aerodynamic design," or "road-gripping tire tread."

Reviewing the final results, I was pleased to find that given the incentive and a little extra practice, my students could both recognize and write topic sentences and descriptive supporting details.

Fran Jeffries, James Wood High School, Winchester, Virginia

Describing the Patter of Little Feet

I have several ideas I use to encourage my middle-school students to use the thesaurus and broaden their vocabularies.

On the bulletin board or chalkboard I tack up or print the words "The patter of little feet. . . ." Above this caption I tack up or draw a pair of footprints. Underneath the word *patter* I list additional words such as *drumming, whisper,* and *reverberation.* I ask students to use their imaginations as well as copies of the thesaurus to come up with other words that suggest sound or noise, and I list these on the bulletin board as well. Then I read the substitutes for *patter* and ask students

to suggest the type of feet that would make the noise suggested by each word—"angry feet," "dancing feet," "giant feet," and so on. Discussing shades of meaning among the synonyms helps students add the words to memory. Next, I list each suggested type of feet next to the noise these feet would make. To help convey the nuances of the suggested words, students take turns drawing and cutting out feet to match the newly created phrases.

When we have exhausted the possibilities in the above idea, I continue the focus on synonyms by running a path of adding machine tape from a pair of feet on the bulletin board, over the file cabinet, under the chalkboard, and along the wall. I write a synonym for *walked* every foot or so for the first few feet, including such words as *sashayed, clumped, sauntered, tiptoed,* and *waddled.* Beside each word, on the wall above or below the adding machine tape, I tape cutouts of a pair of feet. I tell students that anyone who adds a new synonym to the list may also add cutouts of their own feet to the path. Students dig deeply into their copies of the thesaurus for unusual words. In the process, they tend to find not only the targeted words but fascinating words that they can't resist telling to the rest of the class. I encourage this by donating a corner of the board for miscellaneous words that students deem interesting enough to share.

When we run out of room for words and feet on the paper path, we move on to yet another exploration of synonyms. I display on the bulletin board a picture of a warthog, a sloth, or some similarly distinctive creature, bearing the caption: "*I am beautiful,*" *the warthog said.* With students' by-now-expert help, *beautiful* and *said* are soon replaced by less trite and more interesting words such as *entrancing, curvaceous, appealing, winsome,* and *murmured, declaimed, asserted.*

For word searches that introduce a myriad of words for character traits, "It's nice to be polite" opens up rich and often humorous possibilities for word substitution, as does "Today my teacher is cranky." (I recommend the latter for use only by the courageous—or foolhardy—teacher with a thick skin and a secure self-esteem.)

The keen competition between classes to find the most new words and the most interesting words makes all of these tactics highly motivating. Follow-up exercises can prompt students to use the newly learned words in ways that ensure their place in memory.

Margaret G. Dukes, Nimitz Middle School, San Antonio, Texas

Journal Topics for the Jaded

Tired of students' bored responses to the same old journal topics? My students have enjoyed writing in their journals much more since I distributed a list of less-than-traditional writing topics. Some of these are my own, and others are adaptations of familiar topics.

Invent a new "gummy" candy and describe how you would market it.

How has your birth order in your family made you the person you are today?

If it were technologically feasible, would you give men the option of bearing children? Why or why not?

If you could have another eye, where would you have it placed and why?

Write down a joke in exactly the same words as if you were telling it aloud.

Think up and describe a new use for an old appliance.

Have you heard a new album or cassette of music lately? Describe one of the songs in such a way that I can almost hear it.

What was the last thing you heard about or learned that really astonished you?

Describe a current television or radio commercial that you find irritating.

If you could change one law, what law would it be and how would you change it?

Tonnie Hamblin, Hugoton High School, Kansas

Easing Those First-Day Blues

The first day of students' freshman year often causes anxiety and upset stomachs. They come into my classroom as shrinking, invisible shadows, not at all in a frame of mind conducive to learning. Trying for a change of mood, I suggest to students:

Relax. Think back to the most satisfying, successful day you have ever had in school—a day when you presented an oral report and everyone loved it, or when you impressed the class with something you made, or when your teacher told you your short story was one of the best she had read in a long time. Concentrate on how you felt and write a description of that moment.

Soon the room is quiet, heads are bent over pens and paper, and the fear evaporates.

When most students are finished, I encourage a volunteer to tell me something about the moment he or she described. Other students join in, and the mood becomes comfortable and relaxed. As the period draws to a close, I ask students to write another short writing that night for homework—a description of what they felt on their first day of high school. I ask students to include specific details about what they remember most vividly, whether it's what they ate for lunch, the crowds in the hallways, getting lost on the way to class, and so on. I mention that these writings will be brought out again in the spring, and immediately students guess that the second phase of the assignment will be a comparison paper.

Before students turn in the assignment the next day, I ask for volunteers to read parts of their papers aloud. We discuss why they felt afraid and what causes frightening rumors about high school, and then I ask them to try to predict how they will feel in the spring. I read two or three first-day papers from former students (who, I assure my students, made it through high school without major disasters) to demonstrate how universal their feelings are. I collect the papers, write comments, correct major errors, and hand the papers back to students, asking that they return the papers to me when they are finished rereading the assignments.

Then, months later, on a warm spring day, I return the papers to students once again. In their current writing groups, students talk about their memories of that first day. "I can't believe I wrote that," someone always says. The present assignment is to write a paper comparing how they felt then to how they feel now, including thoughts about what has been different from what they expected, what has been the same, and what advice they would give to incoming freshmen.

I have another, similar, idea that I plan to use next year. I will have each incoming student write a letter to an unknown, future freshman from the following year, decribing thoughts and feelings about the first day of school and making predictions for the year to come. In the spring, my students will write follow-up letters explaining how their feelings have changed, telling which predictions turned out to be right and which wrong, and reassuring the first-day freshmen. The next year, when I deliver these "before" and "after" letters to incoming freshmen, they will learn not only of the worries and fears of the previous year's freshmen, but also of friends made, confidence gained, and the good luck wishes of students who went through the same experience.

Ruth Berdick, Glenbrook North High School, Northbrook, Illinois